Southern Gospel Piano

Songs of Faith

Darrell Archer

Online Audio

To access the online audio go to:
WWW.MELBAY.COM/30960MEB

WWW.MELBAY.COM

PREFACE

Southern Gospel Piano - Songs of Faith is perfect for the keyboardist who wants to add a country gospel flair to their presentation of these traditional favorites. These down-home renditions of such songs as "Abide with Me", "Never Alone" and "Blessed Assurance" along with six other well-known hymns and gospel gems are inspiring and enjoyable to play. They are heartfelt, moving and are sure to be appreciated by all.

This piano collection features favorite sacred selections arranged in the bent-note gospel style and are presented in a fresh, creative manner, making this appealing style of playing accessible to those pianists who previously have not had the opportunity or repertoire to pursue this genre of piano music.

While not for the beginner, these pieces are still fairly easy to prepare and present. The results of a little patience and practice are worth the effort expended, so enjoy these *Songs of Faith* arranged in the Southern Gospel piano tradition.

Darrell Archer

CONTENTS

ABIDE WITH ME

HENRY F. BYTE

WILLIAM H. MONK
Arr. Darrell V. Archer

1

Moderately Slow ♪ = 180

F/A Gm C7 Dm7 G7 C Gm
13
18
Am/C C7 F Am/C C♯°7 Dm
17
F7/C B♭ D+ D7/F♯ Gm
21
26
Gm7 C7 F C7 F A7/E
25

29
Dm
Gm
F/C
C7
F
34
33
Cm9
F7
B♭
p
Dm
A°
Gm
37
Dm
E♭
mp
F7
Am7(♭5)
B♭
42
41
B♭
E♭
B♭
E♭

B♭ Cm7 F7 B♭ C7 F Dm
poco rit.
50
Em/G G7 C E E7
mf
a tempo
Am C7 F A7+ A7
8va
(8va)
58
Dm G C G7/B
mp

C E7/B Am Dm C/G G7 C
60
66
G7 C G9 C/G G♯°7
65
mf
Am Fm/A♭ C/G G7
69
F C
8va
73
rit. e dim.
much slower
pp

ALLELUIA! SING TO JESUS

WILLIAM C. DIX

ROWLAND H. PRICHARD

Arr. Darrell V. Archer

2

moderato ♩ = 90

13
8va
F
F2
F
F2
F
F2
Gm
Gm7
(8va)
C/E
F/C
C7
F
B♭/F
F
Gm7
C7/F
21
(8va)
F
Am
Dm7
f
Gm
Gm(maj7)
Gm7
C9
Am/C
C9
F
Dm

29
8va
Gm Gm9 C7 F
(8va)
Gm Em7(♭5) C9 F Dm7 Em7(♭5) C7
F F7 B♭ Am/C Gm/D F F/C C7 F
mf
E♭ G F

40
G
C96
G
F6
f
8va
tacet
44
mp
48
G
C
G
Em/A
G/B
C
G
f
F
51
tacet
3
3
mp

56
54
C
f
Em
Dm
G9
Em/G
G7
C
57
Am7
Dm7
Dm9
G7
61
64
C
mf
G7
C

G7
C
F
C/F
F
72
C/G
G7
C
C/G
C
dim.
mp
B♭
C
8va
B♭
f
15ma
8va
C
poco a poco dim. e rit.

BLESSED ASSURANCE

FANNY J. CROSBY

PHOEBE P. KNAPP
Arr. Darrell V. Archer

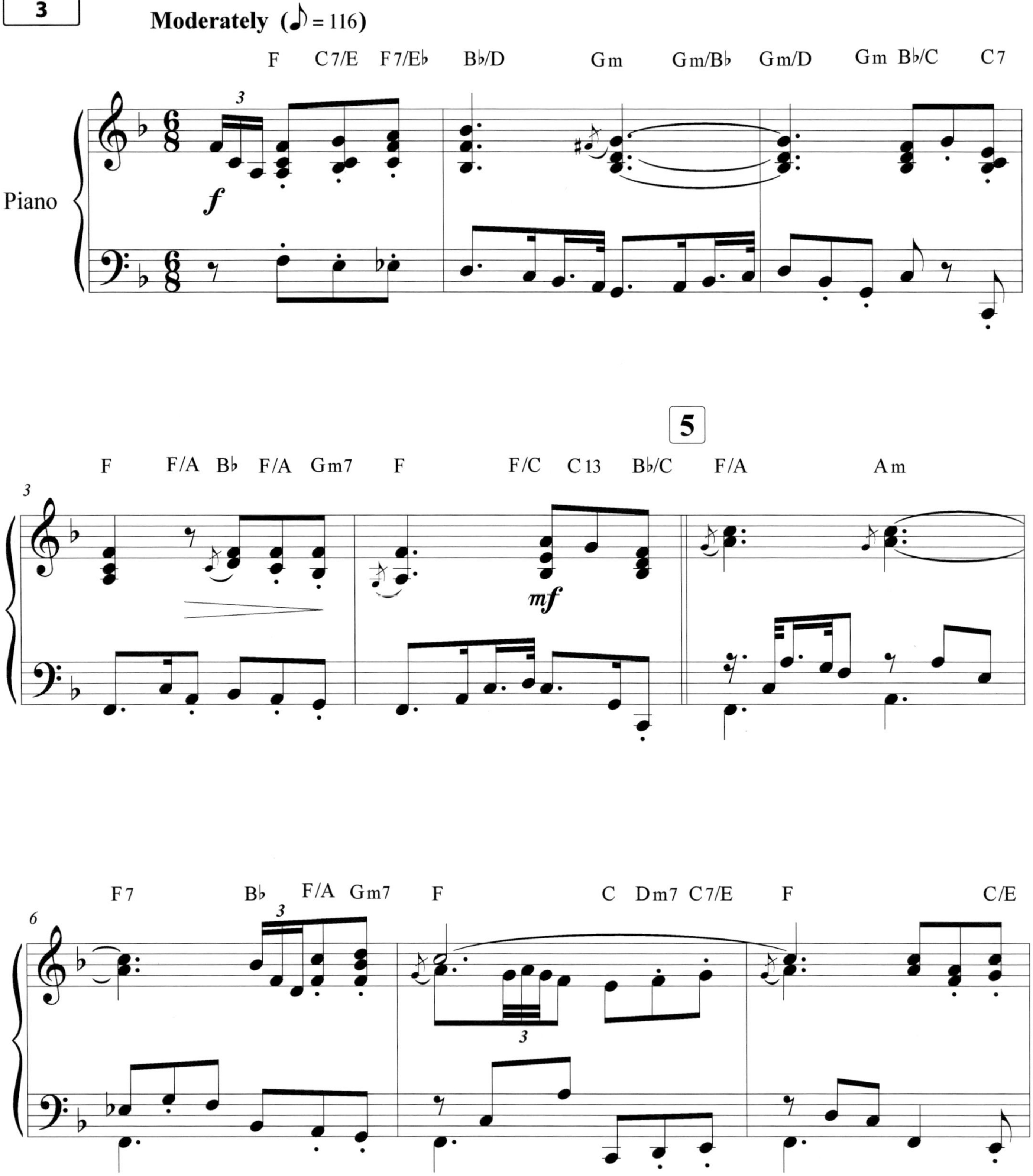

Dm C C/E C Am7 G7 Am G7/B
9
C C/G G13 Em/A G7/B C7 B♭/C F Am
13
11
3
F7 B♭ F/A Gm7 F C Dm7 C7/E F C7/E F7/E♭
14
mp
B♭/D Gm Gm/B♭ Gm/D Gm B♭/C C7 F F/A B♭ F/A Gm7
17

21
F C Dm7 C7/E F F/A F F/C F F7/E♭ B♭ B♭/D
mf
To Coda
F C Dm7 C7/E F F/C F C/E Dm Dm/G C/G G7/B
29
C C/G G13 Em/A G7/B C7 Gm7 C7 F Am
f
F7 B♭ F/A Gm7 F C Dm7 C7/E F C7/E F7/E♭
dim.
mp

Bb/D Bb Gm Gm/Bb Gm/D Gm Bb/C C7 Dm Dm/C Em/B Em7(b5)/Bb
33
A7 A13 D G Em7 D
36
37
f
p legato
Bm Bm/D A/E F#m E7 E7/G# A A/C# A A13
39
D G Em7 D D/F# D D/A D A7/C# D7/C
41

D.S. al Coda
G/B G Em Em/G D/A A7 D C Dm7 C7/E
Coda
C7 Gm7 C7/B♭
Pno.
46
A♭ D♭ A♭/E♭ D♭/F A♭
A♭ E♭7/G A♭7/G♭ D♭/F D♭ B♭m

A♭ E♭7/G A♭7/G♭ D♭/F D♭ B♭m
poco a poco cresc.
B♭m/D♭ A♭ E♭7/G A♭7/G♭ D♭/F D♭ B♭m
54
A♭/E♭ B♭/E♭ E♭7 A♭ D♭ A♭/E♭ B♭m7 C♭ G♭/B♭ A♭m7
ff
molto rit. e dim.
A E/G♯ F♯m7 A♭
8va

CLOSE TO THEE

FANNY J. CROSBY

SILAS J. VAIL
Arr. Darrell V. Archer

Second time to
Am/G G D/A A13 D
13 Even 8ths
Em A7 D D/A Em/G F♯m Bm
cresc.
mf
Em A7 D F♯m/A D7 Am/G G
Shuffle
D.C. al Coda
D/A A13 D

Coda
22
Even 8ths
B♭7
8va
(N.C.)
E♭
B♭7
E♭
Gm
Cm
Fm
B♭7
(N.C.)
E♭
E♭7
A♭
E♭
B♭
30
E♭
E♭7
A♭
mp
Cm7
Fm7
B♭m7
E♭
A♭
A♭7
mf

35
D♭
A♭
A♭/E♭
E♭7
A♭
poco rit.
38
8va
C m/E♭
A♭7
E♭m/G♭
D♭
A♭/E♭
E♭13
A♭
Shuffle
Even 8ths
Slower
mp
3
42
D♭/A♭
B♭m7
A maj7
A♭
molto rit.

THE CHURCH'S ONE FOUNDATION

SAMUEL J. STONE

SAMUEL S. WESLEY
Arr. Darrell V. Archer

13
Eb Bb7/F Eb/G Ab Ab Eb Cm Cm/G G7/D Cm/Eb C/E
mf
16
Fm Bb7/D Eb(addF) Eb/D Ab/C Eb7/Bb Abmaj7 Ab6 Ab
mp
19
Fm7 Fm/C Eb/Bb Bb7 Eb Dm7 Dm7b5 G7
Rhythm Tacet
molto. rit.
22
Rhythm Tacet

G7 C E7+ E B°7 F/A C/G
mf
F G7/D C/E Am/C G/D Dm7 G7/D G7
30
Cmaj7 Dm7 Em7 Fmaj7
Broader
poco rit.
f
Dm7 G9 C/E Am7 Am E7/B Am/C A/C♯ Dm7 D C B A G7 G7/B
C F C Fmaj7 A Fmaj7 C Dm AG Dm7 F E Dm7 F/A F/G G7
mf

38
C
C7
F
Dm
C/G
Am
N.C.
G7(♭9)
37
f
C
A♭
D♭6
40
rit. e cresc.
C
42
8va
ff

THE HAVEN OF REST

HENRY L. GILMORE

GEORGE D. MOORE
Arr. Darrell V. Archer

13
8va
Gm/C Gm B♭6 C7 F
11
(8va)
A+ B♭ F
14
Dm D♭7 F/C C9 F B♭
17
F E♭/G F7/A 21 B♭ E♭9
20
mf

23
F
Fmaj7
F6
F
A7/E
Dm
Dm/A
26
G7
Am7
Bm7(♭5)
C7
Gm
C
Gm7
C7
29
F
C+
F9
F7(♯9)
B♭7
mp
32
F
F/C
Am
Dm
B♭7
F
C9

F F7/C Cm7 F7 B♭sus B♭sus/F B♭sus
B♭13 B♭7 39 E♭ E♭m E♭m6
cresc. mf mf
B♭ D7/F♯ Gm Gm(maj7) Gm7
C7 C9 Cm7 Cm A♭7
poco a poco cresc.

47
D♭
F+
G♭
f
50
D♭
B♭m
A7
D♭/A♭
A♭7
(♭)
53
B♭m
B♭m7
A7/E
A7
55
♪ = ♪
D
F♯+
G
ff
3

58
D
Bm
B♭+
D/A
Em/A
A7
molto rit.
8va
61
D
G
62
D
a tempo
poco a poco rit. e dim.
63
pp

THE SOLID ROCK

EDWARD MOTE

WILLIAM B. BRADBURY
Arr. Darrell V. Archer

B E7 A F♯m E/B B7 E B7
10
E B/F♯ E E/G♯ A F♯m B9 E C♯m
13
f
E/B B/D♯ B7 E C♯m Bsus B7 E
16
mf
20
C C7 F F/C C7 F
19
f

B♭ Gm7 F/C C7 F C7 F
22
F/C C F7 B♭ Gm7 F/C C7 F F7
25
28
B♭ B♭/D E♭ Cm7 B♭/F B♭ B♭/D
B♭/F Gm/B♭ F/A F7 B♭ Gm Gm7 F/A F7 B♭ C7
31
mf
rit. e cresc.
f

34
F
Dm
Gm7
C7
F
slower
37
F
G♭
F
40
E♭
C7
F
molto rit.

WHEN I SURVEY THE WONDROUS CROSS

ISAAC WATTS

LOWELL MASON
Arr. Darrell V. Archer

8

Leisurely ♩ = 78

10
F/C F/D C E7/B Am Bm/D D7/A Dm9 Dm/A G7
13
C G7 C G/B C F/C C Dm/A
16
C C/G E Am Am/E
19
Dm Dm/A C/G G7 C Gm7 C7

22
F C7 F C7 F B♭ F C
mf
25
F B♭/F F/C A7/C♯
mp
28
Dm Em/G G9/D Gm Gm/D C7 F C7
mf
31
F C7 F B♭ F C F

34
A7 A7/C♯ Dm
Gm
Am/C C7
mp
38
37
F
D♭
F7 B♭m
f
40
E♭m
Fm/A♭ A♭7
G G/D
G
poco a poco rit. e dim.
p

NEVER ALONE

SOURCE UNKNOWN

Arr. Darrell V. Archer

B♭ B♭/F G°7 F7/A B♭ B♭/F B♭ G°7 B♭ D7
E♭ B♭ Gm7 F
Second time to CODA
F7 F7sus/C F7 B♭ B♭/F
8va
B♭ B♭/F B♭ G°7 B♭ D7 E♭
mf

(8va)
B♭
F 7
(8va)
B♭
B♭/F
B♭
B♭/F
B♭
G°7
B♭
A♭7(♭5)
E♭
B♭
D.C. al 𝄌
F
F 7
F 7sus
C
F 7
B♭
B♭/F
mp
mf

CODA
B♭
Dm
Dm7
G7
35
poco a poco rit.
p
C
Csus2
C/G
C
E7
F
Fsus2
F
37
a tempo
mf
C
F/C
C/G
C
Am
G7
G7/D
G
G7/D
40
f
G
G7/D
G7
C/G
C
Csus2
C/G
43
mf

C
E7
F
Fsus2
F
C
F/C C/G
C
Am
46
G7
G7/D
G
G7/D
G7
G7/D
G7
49
f
C
F
C/E
Dm7
C
52
3
rit. e dim.
mp